BASIC PRINCIPLES OF POLITICS

by

Francisco José Moreno

Second Edition

CREATIVE ARTS BOOK COMPANY
Berkeley, California • 2000

For information contact:
Creative Arts Book Company
833 Bancroft Way
Berkeley, California 94710
(800) 848-7789

ISBN 0-88739-340-3

Library of Congress Catalog Number 00-102474

Printed in the United States of America

To my son Alejandro

TABLE OF CONTENTS

BASIC PRINCIPLES OF POLITICS

Preface to the Second Edition

Changes in this edition have been limited to altering the order of a few of the principles, to the addition of some quotations, to minor corrections aimed at increasing the clarity and precision of the text, and to the rectification of typographical errors.

I would also like to use this preface to the second edition to convey my appreciation to all who communicated to me their reactions to the first edition of *Basic Principles of Politics* since it is only through the exchange of ideas that understanding of any subject advances.

Foreword

This book is about how politics is, not about how we wish it to be or think it should be.

As we approach a new millennium, our vision of politics continues to be mired in distorted modes of thought and the logic we apply to it remains closer to religion and delusion than to observation and analysis. The principles presented here correspond to fundamental political relationships, institutions, and behavior, and relate to politics much as the principles of physics relate to mechanics: physicists set the boundaries for what can be expected and it is up to the engineers to design and operate the system. Therefore, the principles put forward in this book do not constitute a blueprint for action but an exposition of the parameters within which political action takes place.

As a citizen, I am not devoid of political preferences, but just as a doctor does not render a diagnosis on the basis of his feelings for the patient, as a student of politics, I must report what I see and not what I would like to see or think I should see. Even if the aim were primarily therapeutic, impairing our vision with wishful thinking or preconceived notions can only hurt our ability to perceive accurately what we are observing. Whatever our political goals and hopes, obfuscating, tainting, or falsifying reality to have our druthers is analytically flawed and ethically reproachable.

I have been involved with politics, as participant and observer, for over forty years. I have been, in chronological order, student leader, party activist, union official, member of the underground, prisoner, exile, soldier, teacher and researcher, university administrator, senior executive for one of the world's largest corporations, consultant to political parties, adviser to heads of government, and writer. To what extent my experiences are responsible for my perception of politics, I do not know, but I like to believe they have provided me with various perspectives from which to observe politics and have exposed me to circumstances that prodded my inquisitiveness and sharpened my vision.

When it comes to politics, we tend to interpret rather than observe; we see what we want to see and try to explain the absence of what we think should have been there by ignoring or distorting what is in front of our eyes. The short and terse form in which the principles are presented in this book is not a negation of their complexity, but an effort to redress the balance between what we see and what we pretend to see.

My objective, therefore, is neither interpretation nor advocacy, but description. The principles offered here shall stand or fall not on whether they fit theoretical preconceptions or ideological predilections, but on their ability to help us perceive, clarify, and foresee political events.

There is one sin: to call a green leaf gray...

G. K. Chesterton

THE FEW AND THE MANY

1. Those who make the decisions rule.

2. Societies are organized on an unequal basis—the few making the decisions that affect the many.
   "Nothing appears more surprising to those who consider human affairs with the philosophical eye, than the easiness with which the many are governed by the few."
   David Hume, First Principle of Government, Essays, 1742.

3. The exact number of the few, their extraction, the way they become decision-makers, their style of ruling, and the reasons they give to justify their rule, change. What does not change is the fact that the few rule the many.
   "All communities divide themselves into the few and the many."
   Alexander Hamilton,
   Speeches in the Federal Convention, 1780.

4. The ruling few may come from one or more segments of the community, their tenure may be brief or prolonged, their claim to rule accepted

or contested, the circumstances under which
they rule peaceful or violent, their replacement
harmonious or controversial, but the few always
remain a few.

5. **Power begets privilege.**
    The few making the decisions enjoy more than
    their proportionate share of the good things of
    life—whatever the good things of life may be in
    their communities.

PERSUASION AND COERCION

6. The few have two ways of getting their decisions obeyed: through persuasion and through coercion.

7. To persuade is to dispose a person to do on his own what the persuader wants him to do.

    The persuaded integrates the directives of the persuader into his own will and believes that what he has been persuaded to do is the result of his own volition.

8. To coerce is to force a person to do what someone else wants him to do.

    Coercion is the application of overt pressure on the coerced to force him to do what the coercer wants. Coercion is primarily based on, but not limited to, violence. It can be based on anything the coerced values: prestige, position, money, affection.

    The coerced does under duress what the coercer wants him to do.

9. **The less aware the persuaded is that he is being persuaded, the more effective the persuasion.**
    The more overt the effort to influence someone else's mind, the greater the chance of failure.

10. **The more reluctant the coerced is to do what the coercer wants, the greater the pressure the coercer has to apply.**

11. **Persuasion is more effective than coercion. The former fosters acceptance, the latter imposes submission.**

12. **The persuaded polices himself.**
    Persuasion produces willing and lasting compliance. The persuaded develops an inner disposition to do what he has been persuaded to do. Therefore, when persuasion is achieved, the task of the persuader is complete.

13. **Coercion produces reluctant and temporary compliance.**
    Coercion requires constant renewal. When coercion ceases, the coerced is no longer disposed to do what the coercer wants. The task of the coercer is never complete.

POWER

14. Politics is the competition for power.

15. Power is having one's decisions obeyed.

16. Power vacuums are always filled.

    Political power is a constant. Power vacuums are
    passing occurrences, transitions between waning
    and emerging arrangements, and as one wielder
    of power disappears, another emerges. This
    replacement can result from consensus, competi-
    tion, or imposition, and the transition can be
    smooth or rough, but the power void is invari-
    ably filled.

17. Political power is not limited to government.

    The few making the decisions, wielding power,
    are dispersed throughout the community. With
    the explosive growth of government in modern
    times, more and more of them are found in gov-
    ernment, but they have never all been, nor are
    they all now, in government.

18. Political power rests on persuasion, coercion or
    both; its nature depends on how much it rests
    on one or the other.

19. Political power can be accepted or imposed: it is
    accepted when it rests on persuasion, imposed
    when it rests on coercion.

20. Accepted political power exists when the many
    are persuaded into obedience.
    Accepted political power is the result of the
    many believing the few have the right to rule
    them.

21. Imposed political power exists when the many
    are intimidated into obedience
    Imposed political power is the result of the few
    forcing their rule upon the many.

22. Accepted political power requires agreement
    between what the few order and the many
    believe.
    The key to accepted political power is the fit
    between the commands of the few and the
    beliefs and dispositions of the many. The com-
    mands of the few, to be willingly obeyed, must
    be consonant with the beliefs of the many.

23. **Imposed political power results from disagreement between what the few order and the many believe.**

    When the commands of the few are not in accordance with the beliefs and dispositions of the many, the few can only rule through coercion.

24. **The few have political power in direct proportion to the degree to which their decisions are obeyed.**

25. **Accepted power is efficient.**

    When accepted political power exists, the rulers do not have to spend time and energy justifying their power. They just rule.

    See Principles 11 and 12.

26. **Imposed power is inefficient.**

    When political power is imposed and the many are not convinced of the right of the few to rule, challenges to the rule of the few arise. The few then have to spend time and energy justifying and defending their rule.

    See Principles 11 and 13.

27. **Political power when based on persuasion prospers and lasts; when based on coercion it is unreliable and unstable.**

INSTRUMENTS OF POWER

28. Ideas, force, and money are, in that order, the main instruments of political power.

29. Ideas are the raw material of political persuasion.

30. Force is the basic ingredient of political coercion.

31. Money is a secondary, not a primary, instrument of political power.

    Money can be used in conjunction with persuasion or coercion. As strong as the lure of money is, it fails to generate, by itself, the intensity, commitment, and dedication produced by ideas. And as much as we may like money, the protection of our physical integrity comes before it. When money dominates politics, it is a sign that the rule of the few has weakened and that a struggle for power is forthcoming.

32. The simple possession of ideas or force does not constitute power.

Power is created when an idea or force is applied to making the will of some prevail over the will of others.

33. Ideas and force are not exclusive of one another.

Ideas and force generate different kinds of power, but they can be used together by the ruling few to deal with different segments of the many over whom they rule.

Accepted and imposed power can, and do, coexist.

See Principle 18.

THE POLITICAL SYSTEM

34. The political system is the mechanism of collective indoctrination.

35. The political system consists of all the ideas, relationships, and institutions that contribute to having the rule of the few accepted by the many.

36. The function of the political system is to instill beliefs and create dispositions that support the rule of the few.

    To perform this function, the political system inculcates uniform beliefs and dispositions in the potentially active members of the community.

37. The ideas, relationships, and institutions that constitute the political system perform other functions simultaneously with their political ones.

    Family and school, for example, inculcate beliefs and dispositions in children while teaching them specific skills and acceptable patterns of social behavior.

38. A political system is effective when the ideas, relationships, and institutions which constitute it are mutually supportive.

39. A political system is ineffective when the ideas, relationships, and institutions which constitute it are in conflict and are not mutually supportive.

40. The more uniform the beliefs and dispositions of the community, or of its politically active members, the more effective the political system.

41. The effectiveness of the political system is determined by its ability to preserve and protect the rule of the few.

42. An effective political system is the exception, not the rule.

    Most contemporary communities do not possess effective political systems.

INDOCTRINATION AND PROPAGANDA

43. **The political system works through indoctrination and propaganda.**

    See Principles 34 and 36.

44. **Indoctrination is the inculcation of values and beliefs.**

    Political indoctrination is the instillment of the ideas and dispositions that determine attitude and shape action.

    See Principle 36.

45. **Political indoctrination is carried out by social, not government, institutions.**

    Family, friends, schools, peer groups, and the communication media are the main political indoctrinators.

    See Principle 37.

46. **Propaganda is short-term overt manipulation of information.**
Propaganda is the management of information to attain immediate and specific ends.
The effectiveness of propaganda depends on the degree to which the manipulation of information is consonant with existing beliefs and dispositions.
All communication aimed at creating support for specific proposals, actions, policies, individuals, or institutions is propaganda.

47. **When propaganda fits in with accepted beliefs and existing dispositions, it is not perceived as propaganda.**
Indoctrination and propaganda work in tandem.
Propaganda, to be effective, must build on the beliefs and dispositions of those being propagandized; hence, effective propaganda requires an indoctrinated community.
When out of tune with community beliefs and dispositions, propaganda is reduced to short-term machination.
See Principle 22.

48. **Propaganda can complement indoctrination but it cannot replace it.**

    In an effectively indoctrinated community, propaganda directs shared beliefs and uniform dispositions into specific action.

    In a community that has not been effectively indoctrinated, the efficacy of propaganda is limited.

    Propaganda cannot substitute for the political system.

49. **Communication media and government are the major dispensers of political propaganda.**

    Media comprises all dispensers of mass information and news: the press as well as the publishing and entertainment industries.

50. **What turns information into indoctrination or propaganda is not whether the information is factual, conjectural, or fictional, but the purpose to which it is put.**

    When the transmission of information is limited to verifiable facts, with no explicit or implicit attempt to influence its perception, it is communication. When the transmission of information is done with the intention of molding beliefs, creating dispositions, or directing action, it is indoctrination or propaganda.

51. **The effect of the information transmitted does not depend on its truthfulness.**
    What makes information politically relevant is how it is used by the rulers and how it affects the ruled. Whether such information is eventually corroborated or not is of little consequence.

52. **The less aware the indoctrinator and the propagandist are of what they are doing, the more effective their work.**
    See Principle 9.

53. **A political system is as smooth-running as its propaganda is rooted in effective indoctrination.**
    See Principle 38.

54. **In politics emotion always triumphs over reason.**
    Our emotions are determined by our dispositions and justified by our beliefs.

    "What matters about political ideas is the underlying emotions, the music to which ideas are a mere libretto, often of very inferior quality."
    Lewis Namier, **Personalities and Power,** *1955.*

55. **Reason influences political opinion in inverse proportion to the subjective importance of the issue under consideration.**

    The higher our emotional involvement with an issue, the more important the issue is to us and the less open we are to questions and disagreements. By the same token, the less we care about an issue, the more receptive we are to different ideas and opinions.

56. **A working political system precludes disagreement.**

    In communities with effective political systems, debates center on form not substance. Conflict is limited to how best to implement the beliefs and dispositions that have been instilled in the community. Questioning those beliefs and dispositions is accepted in theory but precluded in practice.

    When substantive political debate takes place within the community it is an indication of either absence of effective indoctrination or the result of internal dissension.

57. **When the political system deteriorates beyond a certain point, there is no way to preserve it; it continues to deteriorate until it collapses.**

    The point of no return is reached when the political role of the social institutions, their indoctrination and propaganda functions, become manifest and the subject of scrutiny and controversy.

58. **A collapsing political system results in a shift from persuasion to coercion.**

    The collapse of the political system leads to the breakdown of the community unless prevented by coercive government action.

    As effective indoctrination fades, reliance on manipulation through propaganda increases.

FORCE

59. Force is the alternative to indoctrination.

In the absence of persuasion only coercion
secures power.

Force is not limited to violence. It implies any
means by which imposition is carried out.
See Principles 6 and 8.

60. Power based on coercion is inefficient.

Force produces compliance but not acceptance; it
elicits submission but it breeds dissent.

Force produces control for a time, but it fails to
secure it.

"The use of force alone is temporary. It may sub-
due for a moment, but it does not remove the
necessity of subduing again."
Edmund Burke, *Speech on Conciliation with
the American Colonies, 1775.*
See Principles 13, 26, and 27.

61. **Those who rule by force wish they could rule by persuasion.**

Since force is second best to indoctrination, those whose power depends on force would prefer to persuade. In their desire to preserve and protect their power, they are often lured into thinking persuasion can be achieved through propaganda. They are mistaken.

See Principle 48.

THE POLITICAL COMMUNITY

62. A political community is the population living under one government.

Rulers and ruled are both part of the political community.

Individuals sharing the same historical background or cultural heritage may wish to be part of the same political community, but if they do not share the same government—if they are not part of the same set of ruler-ruled and of their respective subsets—for all practical purposes they are not members of the same political community.

63. Political communities are uniform or divergent.

A political community is uniform when its members share beliefs and dispositions. A uniform political community is the result of effective and homogeneous indoctrination.

A political community is divergent when its members do not share beliefs and dispositions. A divergent political community is the result of ineffective or disparate indoctrination.

64. A uniform political community is cohesive.
The members of a uniform political community share beliefs and dispositions and, as a result, support one another's views and actions.

65. A divergent political community lacks cohesion.
The members of a divergent political community do not share beliefs and dispositions and, as a result, do not support one another's views and actions.

66. A divergent political community appears to be uniform if one of its component groups monopolizes power.
If one group has effective control over a divergent political community, itself enjoying cohesion and keeping other groups from power, the community appears to be uniform.

67. Uniform political communities are the exception.
Most contemporary political communities are divergent ones with weak internal cohesion.

GOVERNMENT

68. **Government is the set of institutions through which political power is formalized.**

   In communities with effective political systems, government includes the members of the formal opposition who are, in fact, part of the ruling few.

69. **The power of government is inversely proportional to the cohesion of the community.**

   The more cohesive the community, the less the power of government. When effective political indoctrination is in place, when political control of the many by the few is exercised by an efficient social mechanism, the task of government is limited.

   The less cohesive the community, the greater the power of government. When social institutions do not provide adequate support for the ruling few, government tries to fill the gap and do the work of the whole political system.

70. The power of government varies, but it is never total.

The power of government differs according to the characteristics of its community, but government is never the repository of all political power.

LEGITIMACY AND STABILITY

71. A government is legitimate when it is accepted by the community.
Legitimacy is not a legal abstraction but a political fact.

72. A government is illegitimate when it is not accepted by the community.

73. Legitimacy fosters stability.
When the members of the community accept their government, when they view it as having the right to rule them and feel, therefore, compelled to obey it, then the government has a steady life.
See Principle 56.

74. Illegitimacy fosters instability.
When the members of the community perceive their government as not having the right to rule them, when they obey it out of fear, not conviction, the government leads an unsteady existence.
See Principle 60.

75. **Reliance on force implies illegitimacy.**
    A government that relies on coercion, that forces
    the community to comply with its rule, is not
    able to generate acceptance.

76. **Uniform political communities have legitimate
    and stable governments.**
    This principle refers to governments emanating
    from their own communities. It does not apply
    to communities whose governments are the
    result of external imposition.

77. **Divergent communities have illegitimate and
    unstable government.**

78. **A divergent community can have a stable govern-
    ment only if its political system is monopolized
    by one group.**
    If one segment of the community controls
    indoctrination and the political system to the
    exclusion of the rest, then it is possible for a
    divergent community to resemble a uniform
    one. Such a situation, however, lasts only as long
    as the excluded groups remain excluded. As pre-
    viously excluded groups gain access to social
    institutions and, hence, to the political system,
    conflicts emerge and stability is undermined.
    See Principle 66.

TOOLS OF GOVERNMENT

79. **The main tools of government are propaganda and force.**

    Propaganda and force are supplemented with money.

    See Principles 28 and 31.

80. **When government is part of an effective political system, propaganda is its chief tool.**

    In a working political system the main task of government is to turn beliefs and dispositions into action through the management of information. In such a system, the ritual and symbolic undertakings of government are part of its propaganda machine.

81. **Government propaganda is all activity aimed at getting the community to accept and support the objectives and actions of the government.**

    When the government is part of an effective political system, government propaganda has the support of the social institutions: schools, churches, civic organizations, the press. These nongovernmental institutions are partners in the diffusion and validation of government propaganda.

82. **When government is not part of an effective political system, force is its chief tool.**

Propaganda that is not rooted in indoctrination and supported by social institutions has limited effectiveness.

When propaganda does not provide enough control, government turns to coercion.

See Principle 23.

83. **Force and propaganda are not mutually exclusive.**

Governments can and do use both tools simultaneously. It is the degree to which they rely on one or the other that varies.

See Principle 33.

84. **Government propaganda can be subtle or blatant.**

Government propaganda is subtle when individuals and institutions outside government undertake it. It is blatant when undertaken by government itself.

The effectiveness of government propaganda increases when dispensed under the guise of independent and impartial judgment. The greater the prestige and visibility of the individuals or institutions dispensing the propaganda, the greater its effect.

Subtle propaganda is more effective than blatant propaganda.

85. There is no politics without propaganda.

Propaganda is intrinsic to politics.

No political ideas or goals can be advanced without generating support for them. Even when politics comes to be dominated by force, the justification for that force is attempted through propaganda.

The challengers and enemies of the ruling few, those who aspire to replace them and their ideas, are equally dependent on propaganda for making their case, gathering support, and recruiting followers.

LAW AND JUSTICE

86. **Laws are the rules and regulations governing the community.**

There are two kinds of law: written and unwritten.

Written, or formal, law is what the government enacts. Unwritten, or informal, law is what the community enforces—its beliefs and dispositions.

When a judge condemns a thief, he is applying the written law. When someone is granted or denied opportunity or recognition because the way he looks, dresses, or speaks, the unwritten law is being enforced.

87. **Law has two primary functions: to preserve the rule of the few and to protect the physical integrity of the community.**

Law can only perform these functions effectively when its dictates are complementary to the beliefs and dispositions of the community.

All other functions ascribed to law are abstract lucubrations which have little to do with, and often undermine, its primary functions.

88. **Written law that is not consonant with the beliefs and dispositions of the community becomes oppressive.**

    Separate from the beliefs and dispositions of the community, the written law is an empty shell at the mercy of ideologues and practitioners of the legal trade.

    Discrepancy between what the community believes and what the law prescribes breeds disregard for the law, alienation from the government, and dissension.

89. **Justice is an ideological abstraction.**

    Abstract interpretations of justice are ideological statements since justice is always understood in terms of the values held by those defining it.

90. **Law based on abstract concepts of justice is either legal sorcery or doctrinaire gibberish.**

    Using law to promote behavior that is not founded on the beliefs and dispositions of the community, trying to mold action by legal fiat, is indulging in magic or in ideological double-talk.

THE PRESS

91. The press is a political institution.
As the conveyer and interpreter of information, the press is directly involved in the political process. Its control of the flow of information and its influence on the public perception of issues and individuals make it an active political agent.

92. The press is a dispenser of political propaganda.
The power of the press resides in its ability to influence public opinion: to indoctrinate and propagandize.
The press indoctrinates when it contributes to, or supports, the inculcation of beliefs and dispositions upholding the rule of the few.
The press engages in propaganda through the selection of news items and through the connection it makes between these items and the beliefs and dispositions of the community.
See Principles 37, 45, 49, 50, and 51.

93. The political neutrality of the press is a myth.
By the very nature of the function it performs,

the press is politically partisan. Its claims to objectivity and impartiality are spurious and aim at protecting its political influence and effectiveness as indoctrinator and propagandist.

Unawareness on the part of journalists of the political role they play enhances, rather than reduces, the influence and power of the press.

See Principle 52.

94. The power of the press rests on its reporting, not on its editorials.

The political influence of the press resides in its ability to select, present, manage, and direct information, not on direct advocacy.

95. The press is always censored.

Political censorship is the suppression, selective dissemination, or tingeing of information that affects the rule of the few over the many.

96. The power of the press increases in the absence of an effective political system.

Under an effective political system the press, as part of an integrated mechanism of persuasion, has little independent power; it is one more participant in the indoctrinating process and its propaganda functions are clearly demarcated.

When no effective political system is in place, or when the one in place malfunctions, the press increases its influence as selector of information, shaper of perceptions, and arbiter of public issues.

DEMOCRACY

97. Democracy is government by indoctrination.
Democracy is based on consent. Consent results
from uniformity of beliefs and dispositions.
Democracy exists in culturally uniform communities or in communities where a culturally
cohesive group monopolizes control of the
political system.

**98. Democracy is the government of communities
that have effective political systems.**
See Principles 38, 40, and 41.

99. Democracy is freedom to conform.
When indoctrination has done its work, substantive disagreement does not arise.
When the beliefs and dispositions of the community are uniform, the questioning or challeng-
ing of government is tame and restricted.
The greater the degree of uniformity produced by
indoctrination, the freer the government can
allow its citizens to be since these citizens are
not likely to use their freedom to oppose or

undermine the ruling few.

The government-citizen relationship parallels the parent-child one. When children accept their parents' values, when they behave according to their parents' wishes, parents allow their children leeway. When children violate their parents' wishes, when they behave contrary to their parents' values, parents restrict their children's actions.

"Train up a child in the way he should go, and when he is old he will not depart from it."

Proverbs, *22:6*

"Who controls a man's ideas control the man."

Mao Tsetung

100. Democratic government is legitimate and stable.
Acceptance produces legitimacy.
See Principles 12 *and* 71.
Legitimacy produces stability.
See Principles 56 *and* 73.

DICTATORSHIP

101. Dictatorship is government by force.
Rulers resort to force when they cannot persuade.
Coercion is inferior to persuasion as a mechanism of control.
See Principles 11 and 59.

102. Dictatorship is illegitimate and unstable.
Force produces illegitimacy.
See Principles 13 and 72.
Illegitimacy produces instability.
See Principles 60 and 74.

103. Dictatorial propaganda is not as effective as democratic propaganda.
The propaganda of dictatorship lacks the foundations of effective indoctrination.
Without indoctrination upon which to rest, the propaganda of dictatorships takes the form of blatant manipulation.
See Principles 46, 48, and 53.

ELECTIONS

104. Elections are, above all else, symbolic rituals.
In a political system in working order elections have two functions: the ceremonial sanctioning of government and the renewal of personnel.

105. Elections in democracies do not affect the relationship between the rulers and the ruled.
The better the working order of the political system, the less important elections are. In a working political system the options offered to the electorate are circumscribed to individuals upholding similar values and advocating compatible views. Departures from prevailing beliefs and dispositions are precluded.
In democracies candidates are preselected and prepositioned with the active collaboration of the press. The candidates who dissent from prevailing beliefs and dispositions are ignored or marginalized—marginalization often taking the form of ridicule or portrayal as insignificant or unfit.

106. When elections are real contests between substantive alternatives, the political system is not working.

A meaningful electoral contest takes place only when competing beliefs and dispositions allow substantially different options to emerge; and when elections are contests between substantially different options, the political system is malfunctioning.

107. In communities without an effective political system, elections are confrontational.

When the beliefs and dispositions of the community have not been homogenized through indoctrination and propaganda, conflicting political views emerge and gain force. In these cases the electoral process cannot bridge existing differences since these differences are rooted in competing beliefs and dispositions. Under these circumstances elections are confrontations between contending values and political visions. Rather than filling the gap between divergent positions, elections then contribute to the hardening of stances and to the solidification of discrepancies.

COMPROMISE

108. **Compromise comes about when there is agreement—not disagreement.**

    To arrive at the negotiated solution of a disagreement, to compromise, those disagreeing must agree on something more important to them than what they disagree about. They must also believe that continued disagreement on the less important issue would jeopardize the more important one. It is the desire to protect what they agree on, the something they value more than the subject of disagreement, that impels them to find a solution to their differences.

    If a couple disagrees on what to do on an evening out, they would part company unless they placed a higher value on being together. In that case, it is their shared desire to be together that brings about a compromise.

    Without underlying areas of agreement there is no compromise.

109. **Compromise is the result of our willingness to sacrifice the less important to protect the more important.**

110. **Political compromise results from uniform beliefs and dispositions, not from wisdom and tolerance.**

     Believing willingness to compromise is the outcome of higher virtue, of greater tolerance, or of the superior wisdom and maturity of a given culture is fallacious—and biased.

111. **The more uniform the community, the greater its tendency to compromise.**

     The more numerous and deep-rooted the shared beliefs and dispositions, the more powerful the pressure in the community to solve disagreements without endangering those beliefs and dispositions.

112. **The more divergent the community, the weaker its ability to compromise.**

     The scarcer and weaker the shared beliefs and dispositions in the community, the greater the propensity to confrontation and intransigence.

FREEDOM

113. **Freedom is the existence of choice—real and substantive choice.**

114. **Just doing what we want is not freedom.**
    What we want is the product of our beliefs and dispositions. If we do not have meaningful options, or are incapable of giving these options proper consideration, we are not free, regardless of how much we may want to do what we do.
    A slave, however happy, remains a slave.

115. **Believing we are free and being free are not the same thing.**
    Being free requires the existence of viable alternatives.
    Thinking oneself free requires nothing.

116. **Democracy is not based on freedom.**
    A system resulting from efficient indoctrination and propaganda is neither based on nor conducive to freedom.

117. Freedom flourishes when controls fail.

Freedom prospers under systems that function well enough to provide some legitimacy and stability, but not so well that they eradicate all meaningful differences in the beliefs and dispositions of the community.

Inefficient dictatorships also provide opportunities for freedom to grow. Although the threat of repression is always present in a dictatorship, ineffective coercion—because it is ineffective and because coercion engenders antagonism— promotes alternatives.

118. Increases in freedom are preludes to surges in oppression.

The expansion of freedom is the result of the inefficiency of the political system or of the deterioration of the dictatorship. As freedom grows, the power of the ruling few weakens and as it approaches collapse, freedom simultaneously reaches its zenith and enters a period of decline.

Since power vacuums do not last, the breakdown of a mechanism of control sets the stage for the introduction of a new one.

REVOLUTION

119. Revolutions are conservative movements.
   The function of revolution is to replace weak
   rulers and shaky government with strong rulers
   and firm government.

120. Revolutions are not the work of the oppressed.
   The truly oppressed can be oppressed indefi-
   nitely, their very oppression guaranteeing their
   powerlessness.
   Revolutionaries, to be successful, must have
   resources at their disposal and know how to
   use them. These resources, and the ability to
   put them to work, are only available to those
   already partaking in the benefits of their communities. It is also among these people that
   those bound to gain the most by the creation
   of a new order are found.
   In modern societies revolutions are the work of
   the middle class.

121. Unstable government fosters revolution.
   Unstable governments produce temporary
   power vacuums.
   Revolutions are efforts to fill those vacuums.

122. Revolutions are justified through ideology.

The pursuit of power is always disguised as a lofty effort to attain beneficial goals.

IDEOLOGY

123. Ideology is the ascription of transcendental meaning to the pursuit of power.
An ideology is a set of abstract ideas through which it is pretended to explain political reality in terms of moral values and rational logic. Ideologies are used by those in power as well as by those seeking power.

"So far from a political ideology being the quasi-divine parent of political activity, it turns out to be its earthly stepchild...political activity comes first and political ideology follows after."
Michael Oakeshott, *Political Education*, 1951

124. An ideology can be an instrument of persuasion or a justification for coercion.

125. The power of ideology rests on its ability to sway emotions and capture the imagination.
The rational content of ideology is of secondary and peripheral importance.
See Principle 54.

"The ideology of a ruling class is of little use

47

unless it is accepted by those who are being ruled."

Sir Moses Finley, *Politics in the Ancient World*, 1983

126. **In communities with working political systems one ideology reigns supreme. In divergent communities ideologies compete.**

In the first instance ideology is implied in the beliefs of the community.

In the second instance ideologies are explicitly advocated.

NATIONALISM

127. Nationalism is the exaltation of the political community, its beliefs and its symbols.

Nationalism allows for community definition and identification in terms of differences, real or imaginary, with other communities.

"The specific political distinction to which political actions and motives can be reduced is that between friend and enemy."
Carl Schmitt, *The Concept of the Political*, 1932

128. Nationalism is the most powerful of political ideologies.

Nationalism provides a sense of collective identity and as such it is basic to the cohesion of the community.
No community can retain its cohesion without a strong sense of collective identity.
The power of nationalism springs from its emotional content.

129. Nationalism is the only ideology capable of keeping a community together in the absence of an effective political system.

Nationalism is especially important to divergent communities; without it, these communities have nothing preventing them from drifting apart into their cultural or regional components.

130. **Common language, symbols, and myths are essential to nationalism.**

Without them a common identity cannot arise, flourish, or retain its vigor.

131. **War is the most effective tool of nationalism.**

The threat of war is usually as effective as war itself in bringing a community together.

THE MILITARY

132. The military does not meddle in politics—it is part of it.

> The military is, by its very nature, a political institution
>
> As the monopolizer of force and as symbolic representative of national unity, the military is always in a position to influence the decisions of the community.

133. Political power cannot exist without the support of the military.

> The few, to rule, must have the tacit or express support of those who control the instruments of force.
>
> Those vying for political control either gain the support of the military or must destroy the military to attain their goal.
>
> Destroying the military implies the creation of a new one or its equivalent.

134. Government by the military is government by coercion.

> Military dictatorship, the assumption of direct

government control by the military, implies reliance on coercion and results from inability to rule through persuasion.

Military governments may see themselves as permanent or transitional. In either case military rulers supplement force with propaganda.

IMPERIALISM

135. Powerful nations dominate weaker ones.
   The form of domination changes; the fact of
   domination does not.

136. International political vacuums do not last.
   See Principle 16.

137. Powerful nations are imperial nations.
   Whether they intend it or not, powerful
   nations, by the very existence of their power,
   are imperial.

**138. Imperialism is the imposition of cultural, polit-
   ical, and economic modes by strong nations
   upon weak ones.**
   Imperial nations impose their wills and try to
   impose their beliefs and dispositions on subject
   ones. The former form of imposition faring better than the latter. Without the benefit of paral-
   lel internal indoctrination to lend them support, the beliefs and dispositions imperial
   nations try to export do not take root in alien
   soil—they are either rejected or distorted. What

imperial nations end up imposing on subject ones are rootless structures and formal processes which vanish when the imperial nations' power wanes.

139. Subject nations show their subjugation by aping imperial ones.

The imitation of the powerful testifies to the subject condition of the imitator.

The present popularity of "democratic" regimes responds less to changes in native beliefs and dispositions than to the preponderance of American economic and military power.

140. Imperialism is not dead—it has changed costume.

Contemporary imperialism is domination through communications and economics. Military power is never irrelevant to imperialism, but at present it supports rather than spearheads imperial control. Should military power be removed, however, contemporary imperialism would collapse.

TOTALITARIANISM

141. Totalitarianism is absolute political control.
Trying to obtain absolute control is not the same as obtaining it.
The modern world has known no true totalitarianism but only attempts at it; however, as control over the mechanisms of persuasion get concentrated in fewer and fewer hands, the possibility of totalitarian control increases.

142. The opposite of totalitarianism is freedom.
Freedom exists to the degree that the control of the few over the many is imperfect.
See Principles 113, 114, 115, and 117.

143. Totalitarianism cannot result from coercion.
Coercion can bring about submission but not control of the mind. Without control of the mind totalitarianism is not possible.

"A really efficient totalitarian state would be one in which the all-powerful executive of political bosses and their army of managers control a population of slaves who do not have to be

coerced, because they love their servitude."
Aldous Huxley, **Brave New World,** 1946.

144. Totalitarianism can only result from persuasion.

Total political power can only be attained by
the few by thoroughly dominating the mind
and will of the many. Totalitarianism hence
requires a highly effective political system, a
system based on control through indoctrination and propaganda with the full support of
modern technology.

FASCISM

145. Fascism is the effort to gain absolute control through force and propaganda.

Fascist regimes cannot achieve the total control they are after, but fascist systems can secure effective, widespread, and lasting power.

146. Fascism is the product of modern technology.

Fascism depends on the mobilization and support of a segment of the many to impose the control of the few over the totality of the community.

The mobilization of followers and the imposition of fascist rule over the community is not possible without the efficacy of modern instruments of coercion and means of communication.

147. The ideological differences between fascist regimes are cosmetic; their structural similarities, essential.

The disparate ideological wrappings of fascist movements are different road maps to the same objective. The discrepancies between Nazism

and communism were those of different adver-
tisement campaigns for the same product.

148. The lure of fascism is easily underestimated.
It took World War II to destroy fascism in
Europe and Asia, and the Cold War to undermine its communist version in the Soviet Union
and Eastern Europe.
Fascist regimes have been undone by external,
not internal, forces. This speaks of their strength
once established.

**149. Fascism is not the path to totalitarianism but an
unapt attempt to achieve it.**

**150. The current tendency towards totalitarianism
induces the alternative of fascism.**
As the move towards homogeneous standards
of values and behavior gains momentum, as uniformity increases, negative reactions will take
fascist form.
Increasingly deprived of access to the mechanisms of persuasion, dissenters will be left with
two options: to conform or to rely on force and
propaganda to present and defend their views.

**Since everything lies open to view,
there is nothing to explain.**

Wittgenstein

Afterword

Truth does not imply complete knowledge or exactness. Knowing that something works in a certain manner does not require or mandate familiarity with the details of how it works. We cannot explain the nature of gravity, but no one doubts its existence or its effects. We know that if we do not attend to a bleeding wound we may bleed to death although we may not be able to tell exactly how much blood our body holds or how much of it we can afford to lose.

A principle is the constant that emerges from variation. We know minorities rule majorities, but the specific size of the ruling minority, its proportion to the majority, how it is selected, what segments of the community it comes from, its average age and sex, may vary from one community to the next. However, the fact that the rulers remain a few, that irrespective of variations this does not change, makes it a constant—a principle.

Historical circumstances and cultural peculiarities affect our behavior and the institutions we create. The principles of politics, to the degree they can be detected, are hence bound to manifest themselves differently at different times and under different conditions. The more varied the manifestations, the greater the importance, if we are to understand politics, of separating the constant from the transient—the principle from its modalities.

The forces arrayed against a lucid and dispassionate assessment of our own behavior are formidable. They range from the difficulties of observer and observed being the same, to the limitations our very nature places on our ability to view, gauge, and judge complex phenomena.

Given the magnitude of the obstacles, our disinclination to adhere to straight and clear appraisals of ourselves is understandable. What is less understandable is our persistent attempt to hide our analytical flaws under a thick layer of intellectual pretentiousness and moralistic petulance.

Author's Biography

FRANCISCO JOSÉ MORENO

Mr. Moreno was born in Havana, Cuba, in 1934. After the military coup d'état that overthrew constitutional government in the island in 1952, Mr. Moreno became active in both the political and underground movements opposing the Batista dictatorship. Persecuted by the government police and jailed three times, Mr. Moreno went into exile in the United States and, after serving in the U. S. Army and marrying, became an American citizen.

Mr. Moreno received a Ph. D. from New York University in political science. His first book called attention to the structural weakness of the Chilean political system and foresaw the institutional breakdown that occurred during the

Allende government. After joining the political science department of NYU, Mr. Moreno became a consultant to several governments and political parties. He advised Prime Minister Adolfo Suárez of Spain during the transition from Franco's authoritarian regime to electoral democracy.

In 1980 Mr. Moreno left the academic world and joined Philip Morris as Vice President for international affairs. In 1993 he resigned and has since returned to work as consultant, writer, and teacher.

Mr. Moreno's second book, *Between Faith and Reason*, originally published in 1979, elicited national and international acclaim as "thought-provoking", "superb", "absolutely brilliant", "highly original, full of fascinating ideas, and beautifully executed". A revised edition appeared in 1998.

Mr. Moreno lives in San Francisco, California.

"*Basic Principles of Politics*...is thoughtful, precise, crisp, and well-calculated to provoke discussion."
—Lee C. McDonald, Professor Emeritus, Pomona College

"You have done an excellent job of pulling together many of the most important ideas and principles found in the political sciences...Congratulations on a very nice piece of work."
—Albert Somit, Professor of Political Science,
University of Illinois, and co-author of *Darwinism, Dominance and Democracy*

"It (*Basic Principles of Politics*) is honest—refreshingly candid—and 'manly.' It avoids pedantic jargon. It is insightful...It shows erudition. It is an easy read: no stumbling over what you wrote. It is food for thought and understanding."
—Raymond Polin, Professor Emeritus of Government & Politics, and author of *Plato and Aristotle on Constitutionalism*

"Moreno presents in a concise, direct fashion some of the most impressive theoretical work I have ever seen. This is definitely a book that will always be on my required textbook list."
—Alfred G. Mueller, Professor, Penn State University

"I found (your book) quite interesting . . . and like (your) questioning of political assumptions."
—Naomi Chazan, Professor of Political Science and Deputy Speaker of the Knesset, Israel

". . . (a) dispassionate rethinking of our most basic political ideas. It requires a lot of courage to write in this manner."
—Dircêo Torrecillas Ramos, Professor, Universidade de Sâo Paolo, Brazil

"A good approach to . . . many important political issues, institutions, and ideas . . . congratulations!"
—Werner J. Patzelt, Professor, Institut für Politikwissenschaft, Dresden University, Germany

"I have nothing but high praise and admiration for your work and for your temerity to lay it before a profession awash in jargon, cant, and bureaucratic apparatus as our social science has increasingly become. If enough of us are stirred by the strong implications of what you've offered, there may yet be hope for us. Bravo!"
—John C. Wahlke, Professor Emeritus, University of Arizona

Praise for *Basic Principles of Politics*

"...(a) considerable effort to develop an innovative and critical point of view."
—Leonardo Morlino, Professor, Università degli Studi di Firenze

"...a wonderful book."
—Hiroshi Machida, Takachiho University, Tokyo

"...tremendous food for thought...sensible and lucid..."
—James Fallows, author and former editor of
US News and World Report

"...thought provoking..."
—Graeme Garrard, Cardiff University, Great Britain

"...incisive treatment of the subject...a brilliant exercise in sincerity..."
—Jorge Tallet, philosopher, author of *The Possible Universe*

"I'll recommend the book (*Basic Principles of Politics*) to my graduate students as a rich source of ideas and hypotheses to be explored and tested further."
—Arend Lijphart, author of *Patterns of Democracy* and Professor,
University of California, La Jolla

"I found your principles compelling...There is a winsome novelty in your stark approach to politics."
—James A. Stever, University of Cincinnati

"...most interesting book on politics...struck by the resemblance of your ideas to Bentham in a number of respects..."
—F. Rosen, Co-Editor of *The Collected Works of Jeremy Bentham*
and Professor, University College, London

"Refreshing. It directs us...to the Machiavellian fundamentals in their true sense."
—Sasson Sofer, Director, The Leonard Davis Institute for International
Relations, The Hebrew University of Jerusalem

"If there is such a thing as an academic page turner, your book (*Basic Principles of Politics*) is it. I could not put it down. It is simply absorbing."
—Mostafa Rejai, Distinguished Professor, Miami University,
Ohio